Home

Deliverance

Prayers to Get Rid of Demons, Close Evil Doorways, and Command God's Blessings and Breakthrough in Your Home

Daniel C. Okpara

Copyright © October 2020 by Daniel C. Okpara.

All Rights Reserved. Contents of this book may not be reproduced in any way or by any means without the publisher's written consent, except for brief excerpts in critical reviews and articles.

Published By:

Better Life Media.

BETTER LIFE WORLD OUTREACH CENTER.

Website: www.BetterLifeWorld.org

Email: info@betterlifeworld.org

FOLLOW US ON FACEBOOK

Like our Page on Facebook for updates:

https://facebook.com/danielokparaglobal

This title and others are available for quantity discounts for sale promotions, gifts, and evangelism. Visit our website or email us to get started.

In this book, Scripture quotations are taken from the New King James Version, except where stated—used by permission.

All texts, calls, letters, testimonies, and inquiries are welcome.

Are you looking for resources to keep your spirit on fire?

Follow me on my Facebook (PRIVATE GROUP) for daily 30-minute morning broadcast. Stir your spirit for Jesus every morning. Start and end your day with powerful prayers and teachings and command your breakthrough.

JOIN NOW FOR FREE

https://facebook.com/danielokparaglobal

CONTENTS

Introduction 7

1. Why Deliverance Prayers Over Your Home? 13

2. What is Home Deliverance? 32

3. When to Do Deliverance Prayers In Your Home 40

4. How to Initiate A Home Deliverance Session 48

Day 1: Prayers for Mercy 63

Day 2: Erect a New Altar 68

Day 3: Address the Powers 75

Day 4: Salvation Prayers 83

Day 5: Guidance and Favor 87

Day 6: Protection 101

Day 7: Divine Provision 104

Contact Us 109

Other Books By The Same Author 110

Notes 115

Receive Weekly Prayers

Powerful Prayers Sent to Your Inbox Every Monday

Enter your email address to receive notifications of new posts, prayers and prophetic declarations sent to you by email.

Email Address

Sign Me Up

Go to: BreakThroughPrayers *to subscribe to receive FREE WEEKLY PRAYER POINTS and prophetic declarations by email.*

www.breakthroughprayers.org

FREE BOOKS

Download these four powerful books today for free... take your relationship with God to a new level.

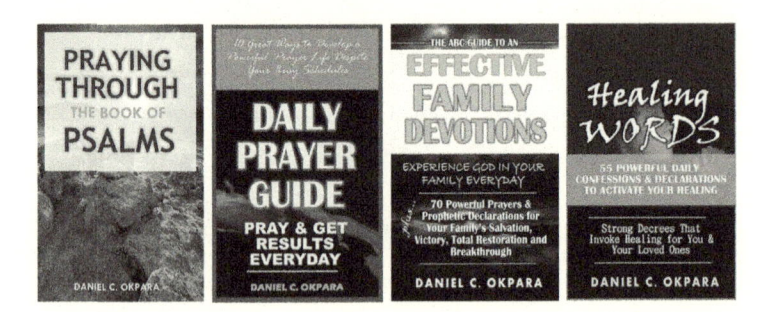

Click Here to Download

www.betterlifeworld.org/grow

INTRODUCTION

₂₅But thus says the Lord: "Even the captives of the mighty shall be taken away, and the prey of the terrible be delivered; for I will contend with him who contends with you, and I will save your children. – Isaiah 49:25

This book provides you with prayers to declare over your home, building and environment and command any form of darkness to cease to exist. But first, is it necessary and important? Can an environment, building or property be under a demonic influence? Aren't demons only able to possess or oppress humans? Should we bother about this whole family deliverance, home cleansing, praying over an environment, and deliverance thing?

Maybe *deliverance ministers* should just shut up and teach people faith. Right?

Well, not so fast.

I understand. There's a genuine reason to be concerned about the topics of demons, deliverance and warfare prayers. However, the challenge with these topics is not the topics themselves because they are, evidently, Biblical realities. The problem comes when people go extreme, magnifying demons and attributing every issue to demons, thus, chasing after demons, morning, afternoon and night.

I always say in church, "Don't spend all your life chasing after demons and deliverance. Demons are fallen angels trying to cause trouble. You've got Jesus Christ. He is the Light that forbids darkness and demons around you."

Nevertheless, this doesn't mean that demons are not real or does not cause bing problems. As I said in my book, **Demonology 101,** *"There's need for balance.*

*"Demons exist for real and have actual powers to wreak havoc and damage. They are not a fabrication of our imaginations. The Bible paints a picture of them as real, evil beings that create real problems, hindrances, and crisis. They are not just **what we think about** and can wish out with motivational, positive thoughts."*

Demons and demonic problems are real. But we need not make them the biggest deals of our lives. When we suspect or identify their activities, operations, projections and attacks, we simply rebuke them in faith, not in fear, cast them out and declare our deliverance and protection in Christ. We are not, as believers, to become demon hunters – chasing demons and talking about how horrible they are dealing with us every day.

With that said, let me bring you into the meat of this prayer book...

DEMONS IN THE HOUSE

Demons can take captive a building, or an environment, and carry out their nefarious activities from that place. I once checked into a hotel where I wanted to stay and meditate. Unfortunately, I had to check out of that hotel as I sensed whoring spirits in that environment.

God is everywhere, yes. But not everywhere is conducive for God's presence.

There are places you will go, and you'll see the spirits of poverty and failure speaking loud and clear. Some places speak witchcraft, death, racism, sodomy, or other demonic corruptions.

Sometimes, environments, buildings, or properties can be a playground of demonic activities. The environments will ooze out so much evil that it will be difficult for occupants of such places to experience peace and breakthrough. Anyone who wants to breakthrough from such an environment must first take charge spiritually.

This book is written to help you understand this mystery in a bold and positive way, and also help you to stand and possess your environment for God, starting from your home.

DON'T FORGET...

"Demons and demonic problems are real. But we need not make them the biggest deals of our lives. When we suspect or identify their activities, operations, projections and attacks, we rebuke them in faith, not in fear, cast them out and declare our deliverance and protection in Christ."

1

WHY DELIVERANCE PRAYERS OVER YOUR HOME?

"The thief does not come except to steal, and to kill, and to destroy. I have come that they may have life and that they may have it more abundantly." – John 10:10

Francis was doing well for himself financially. He was gainfully employed while his wife had a beauty shop with a good number of clienteles. Then they relocated. They packed into another house in another part of the city. It was a bigger apartment where they hoped to have more room and comfort. Unfortunately, things didn't go as they expected.

As soon as they settled in their new apartment, they started noticing mysterious happenings. Sometimes, in the midnight, it would seem as though people were in the sitting room having a discussion. They could hear voices and laughter but not see anyone.

At first, it was Francis who observed the strange happenings. He didn't immediately tell his wife nor the kids. He felt God may be trying to show him things. But then, the wife started having strange nightmares. To have a sound sleep, they must need to pray and pray and pray. Then the kids too. Sometimes, they would suddenly wake up in the middle of the night and start to cry.

After several months, Francis and his wife, Rose, put two and two together, and it dawned on them: this house is under attack.

Then they began to ask questions:

- What happened to the people who packed out of this apartment?

- Are other tenants experiencing the same thing?

- What must have happened in this house that made it a den of demons?

The more they asked questions, the more they discovered that they had packed into a demonized house. But being a minister, Francis decided he was going to take charge. He was going to pray away the demons and claim his peace of mind in the house. He wasn't going to be intimidated and run away. So, he intensified his prayer.

Regrettably, things got worse.

Whenever they prayed so much, the situation would calm but would resume after a few weeks. Remember what Jesus said:

> "When an evil spirit leaves a person, it goes into the desert, seeking rest but finding none. ₄₄Then it says, 'I will return to the person I came from.' So, it returns and finds its former home empty, swept, and in order. ₄₅Then the spirit finds seven other spirits more evil than itself, and they all enter the person and live there. And so that person is worse off than before. That will be the experience of this evil generation." - Matthew 12:43-45 (NLT)

This seemed to be what was happening to Francis' home. Yes, the demons don't have the right and can't possess them, but the demons lay claims over the property they lived in. They would always come back, and things would seem worse afterwards. While demons cannot possess a Christian, they can dwell in an environment and oppress a Christian.

After some time, the demons took the fight to another level. First, Francis lost his job. Then suddenly, customers stopped coming to the wife's shop as they used to. And before long, they began to experience a high level of hardship.

When Francis brought the situation to my attention, I reasoned with him and said, "Maybe this is a needless spiritual battle for you. You do not have a legal authority over that building to relocate the demons. You're a tenant, not the owner. How about finding another apartment?"

"You're right," He said. "But things are now so bad that I don't even have money to rent another place. What am I going to do? My wife's shop is now closed. We couldn't renew the rent, so we were evicted."

To cut a long story short, Francis sold his damaged car, rallied around for financial assistance, and moved out of the house. It's now several months on, he is happy again and has less spiritual warfare to do every night to have a sound sleep. He now has a new job and is gradually taking back everything the demons stole from him.

Hallelujah!

I know. You want to ask many questions:

- Why couldn't he end the demonic assault in the building since he was a man of God?

- Are you saying that demons are stronger than our prayers?

- How about other tenants living there?

- Where is his faith?

The answer to these questions lies in this statement: *"You're not called for every battle."* When you take on battles for which you do not have the spiritual and legal authority, you're bound to fail.

Of course, demons are of lesser power than every Christian. But they understand spiritual laws and rules.

Look at this way: can a tenant evict another tenant in a building?

The answer is no.

Ownership is what confers on anyone the legal right to the possession of a thing. If you rent a property, you do not own that property. There's a limitation to what you can do with the property. While you have the right to the portion of the property you rented, you cannot act as the owner of the entire property. So, when Francis and his family prays, the demons leave their flat. But they still have a hold of the entire building. So, they come back again and again and fight back.

In my over 20 years of ministry, I've come face to face with *demons in a house*. I've seen many oppressed environments, buildings, and properties, and I've seen the damages they can cause for the occupants. When necessary, we must pray over our houses, properties, homes, and environments and declare them safe. Here are three reasons to do that:

1. DEMONS CAN OCCUPY PROPERTIES

Demons and evil spirits can possess animals, buildings, streets, or even objects, and from there cause problems for the occupants or caretakers of those things. This is usually possible where they have been permitted to come and operate. These permissions come in the form of witchcraft activities that took place in those places, blood covenants, animal ritual sacrifices, false worships, cultism, and every form of activity that knowingly or unknowingly invites satan into a place. Look at this story:

> ₁ Then they came to the other side of the sea, to the country of the Gadarenes. ₂ And when He had come out of the boat, immediately there met Him out of the tombs a man with an unclean spirit, ₃ who had his dwelling among the tombs; and no one could bind him, not even with chains, ₄ because he had often been bound with shackles and chains. And the chains had been pulled apart by him, and the shackles broken in pieces; neither could anyone tame him.
>
> ₅ And always, night and day, he was in the mountains and the tombs, crying out and cutting himself with stones.
>
> ₆ When he saw Jesus from afar, he ran and worshipped Him.
>
> ₇ And he cried out with a loud voice and said, "What have I to do with You, Jesus, Son of the Most High God? I implore You by God that You do not torment me."

₈ For He said to him, "Come out of the man, unclean spirit!" ₉ Then He asked him, "What is your name?"

And he answered, saying, "My name is Legion; for we are many." ₁₀ Also he begged Him earnestly that He would not send them out of the country.

₁₁ Now a large herd of swine was feeding there near the mountains. ₁₂ So all the demons begged Him, saying, "Send us to the swine, that we may enter them." ₁₃ And at once Jesus gave them permission. Then the unclean spirits went out and entered the swine (there were about two thousand); the herd ran violently down the steep place into the sea and drowned in the sea. – **Mark 5: 1-13**

The demons in this scenario moved from a human being to animals and then to the sea. I bet that if you had a boat in that sea, at that time, you'd be in trouble, as moving into the sea doesn't mean the demons died.

This story shows that one may not be the direct person involved in an activity that brings demons into a place. But if something has taken place to invite them into an environment, they will be there causing troubles, nonetheless.

The pig owners did not invite the demons to possess their pigs; neither did they do anything wrong that was an attraction for evil spirits at that time. They were simply at the wrong place at the wrong time.

In real-life situations, one may not do anything to bring demons into their environments. But one can be at a wrong place and at a wrong time, and thus, suffer attacks from demons in that particular environment.

Evil spirits can be resident in an environment - buildings, lands, rivers, forests, and so on – even before someone comes there to live. These evil spirits will continue to operate until someone with the spiritual and legal authority tells them: *"Get out of here, in Jesus name."* That's why deliverance prayers should be made over an environment when there is proven suspicion of demonic activity around that environment.

2. CLOSE DEMONIC DOORWAYS

The graven images of their gods you shall burn with fire. You shall not desire the silver or gold that is on them, nor take it for yourselves, lest you be ensnared by it, for it is an abomination to the Lord your God.

Neither shall you bring an abomination (an idol) into your house, lest you become an accursed thing like it; but you shall utterly detest and abhor it, for it is an accursed thing. – Deut. 7:25-26 (AMPC)

Another reason to prayer-cleanse our homes when we sense an influence of darkness around is to locate and close demonic doorways.

Demonic doorways are things that give evil spirits access into a person's house, property or life. These things can be covenants, past occultic activity, past dealings with witchcraft and witch doctors, unholy agreements, using things dedicated to demons, etc.

In the scripture we just read, God tells His people that they will come under a curse and suffer if they bring into their houses things used for idol worship; things like books, drawings, replicas, toys, gifts, jewelry, etc.

In other words, if, in your house, or in the building where you live, things used for satanic rituals and ceremonies are found, you will come **'under the barn'** or curse. And curses produce afflictions, pains and all forms of setbacks.

Yes, you may be innocent and not even know that such a thing had taken place before you acquired the property, or come to live in the building. But your innocence and ignorance do not cancel the reality that the property or the place in question has been a point for some sort of demonic activity.

In the story above, the Israelites suffered because one man had possession of things dedicated or used in idol worship. Until the issue was traced and the doorway found out and removed, they could not confront their opposition and move forward in God's plan for their lives.

You may not genuinely know that an environment was used for some witchcraft activities. But that doesn't stop the fact that the place was used for such activity.

Think about it this way: you do not know that a bottle's content is poison, so you drank it. God will protect you, yes. But that does not mean that the content in that bottle was not poison.

You may not know that an object was used for demonic purposes and bring it into your house. But that does not stop the fact that the object was used for demonic purposes. The contracted and connected spirits in the objects has a legal opening to operate and cause trouble.

Prayer-cleansing our homes helps us to trace every demonic doorway and deal with them. Such doorways can be our attitudes, past actions and activities, past dealings and transactions with the wrong and evil people, objects with demonic influences brought into the house unknowingly, materials, symbols and tools used for some witchcraft occult activity.

"Pastor," you say, "How can we know the exact things that are the doorways for evil spirits into our lives and homes?"

First, it requires the Holy Spirit's leading to tell evil spirits' exact access points into a place or person's life. As we pray with an open mind and seek the Lord, God will lead us to make the right calls and take away what belongs to the devil in our possession.

Second, when we can't find or locate physical objects to remove, we must believe our prayers and not entertain fear. As we pray and declare, somehow, everything that represents demonic doorway will be supernaturally removed.

3. DEDICATE A PLACE TO GOD

When we prayer-cleanse a home, a property, or an environment, we dedicate that home, property and environment to God. That's another reason to do that when necessary.

Dedicating persons, buildings, properties, and belongings to God is a spiritual necessity that the Bible highly recommends. It is a way to proclaim God as the owner of the dedicated thing. We make Him the King, Lord, Savior, Protector, and Preserver of the things we dedicate to Him.

"When something is dedicated to God, it becomes holy unto Him."

When we pray a prayer of cleansing and deliverance over a home or property, what we are saying is:

"Satan, demons, evil spirits, get off his home, get off this property!

"This place belongs to the Lord from now onwards.

"This car, this office, this property, everything here belongs to the Lord.

"Whatever you are holding onto as leverage is, at this moment, destroyed.

"Now leave."

We retake the place for God.

So you see, we have good enough Biblical reasons to pray over our homes and environments when we sense the need to do so.

DON'T FORGET...

"While demons cannot possess a Christian, they can dwell in an environment and oppress a Christian."

2

WHAT IS HOME DELIVERANCE?

Submit yourselves, then, to God. Resist the devil, and he will flee from you – James 4: 7 (NIV)

Home deliverance is the process of setting your habitation and household free from any form of perceived ungodly manifestation, demonic activity, attack, or oppression through spiritual warfare prayers. It is praying and interceding over your family and home environment and commanding supernatural intervention over evil attacks or problems in the family.

There are times you must stand in the gap for your home and family and pray until God's light shines and removes every form of darkness challenging your peace and breakthrough. Sometimes, this can mean standing in the gap and praying for your children and never giving up until hostile powers are broken off their lives. Sometimes, it can mean to stand in the gap and pray for your spouse's spiritual restoration. Sometimes, it can mean to declare over your home continually and force to cease every demonic attack or presence threatening your peace of mind. And sometimes, it can mean to pray and remove your household from discovered negative generational patterns.

A house, a building, an environment, or a home can be under spiritual attack. The people in such houses, buildings, and environments can suffer oppression that produces problems like destructive behaviors, addictions, setbacks, sicknesses, nightmares, and unexplainable persistent hardship. Until the demonic control in such buildings and environments are broken, the occupants of such places will never experience their breakthroughs – healings, peace of mind, financial open door, etc.

YOU ARE A PRIEST IN YOUR HOME

The first vital lesson I teach every time I talk about the home system is reminding us that we are priests and watchmen over our homes (Revelation 1:5). We are not in the homes we belong to by accident.

Nothing happens in life by accident.

God has called you as a priest and a king unto Himself. He strategically placed you in your present home so that you can enforce His will there. You must take spiritual responsibility and begin to decree and declare His will. You cannot stop halfway. You must continue to stand in the gap and speak forth His promises.

The battle in your home is not a physical one. Take your place as God's priest and begin to offer spiritual sacrifices. Begin to decree, declare and command His will to happen. That's how to move all the mountains you see today.

BINDING AND LOOSING

Every Christian must accept the ministry of binding and loosing. Things will not change because you are getting old and tired of your problems. Neither will things change by getting worked up and annoyed about the problems and challenges that confront you.

From time to time, you must learn to rise and say **"*no way*"** whenever things are not going right in your life or home.

God has given us the power and grace to change our lives and circumstances. If you don't resist the devil and stand your ground, he will never flee.

"Stop crying and begging. Start submitting to God and resisting the devil and claiming your victory in Christ."

You can't stop the devil or obtain deliverance for your spouse, children, and home by complaining and wondering why you must go through these many challenges. You can't enforce any change by physically fighting the people trying to hurt you. You must go spiritual. Pick up your arms and start declaring that enough is enough.

WHERE TO START FROM

If you suspect that there is something spiritually wrong in your home, or experience some surge of demonic attacks in the environment where you live or work, or observe a distressing negative generational pattern that continues to manifest, take your spiritual position immediately and start praying to enforce God's will there. Your family is within your spiritual boundary. So, start exercising your spiritual authority.

You can pray and seek deliverance for your family, especially your immediate family, which involves you, your spouse and children. If the situation involves the extended family, you can intercede, but your extended family is not within your direct spiritual authority. All you can do is pray and believe and leave everything in God's hands.

Trying to reach out to extended family members and sharing the need for family deliverance prayer sessions can be very technical and challenging. Don't feel bad if you try and they don't respond. Just start within your spiritual boundary area – your immediate family – and enforce God's will through persistent warfare prayers.

Start where you are right now and bein to invoke God's deliverance and restoration. God will do what He hears you say. Your prayers will be answered.

DON'T FORGET…

"The battle in your home is not a physical one. Take your place as God's priest and begin to offer spiritual sacrifices. Begin to decree, declare and command His will to happen. That's how to move all the mountains you see."

3

WHEN TO DO DELIVERANCE PRAYERS IN YOUR HOME

₁₁Put on the whole armor of God, that you may be able to stand against the wiles of the devil. ₁₂For we do not wrestle against flesh and blood, but against principalities, against powers, against the rulers of the darkness of this age, against spiritual hosts of wickedness in the heavenly places. ₁₃Therefore take up the whole armor of God, that you may be able to withstand in the evil day, and having done all, to stand. – Eph. 6: 11-13

So, now you know why it is important to carry out deliverance prayers over your home or property. Here are three occasions when you must initiate these prayers.

1. NEW PROPERTY

If you are moving into a new apartment, a new office, or taking possession of a new land you purchased, there is no better time to cleanse the property of unknown activities of darkness than this time. Come in the place of prayer and command any evil spirit hiding in such property using the evil doings of the first occupiers of the land or property as an entry point to get off.

You can command whatever is not of the Lord to disappear from your property and rededicate the house, building, property to the Lord and declare it *a no go area for the devil.*

2. SPIRITUAL ATTACKS

There are common warning signs that your home or property is under attack. When you notice those signs, you must arise and raise the banner of victory over the environment through prayers and scripture-declarations. Inability to understand and command the evil manifestations to be neutralized can result in something worse than expected. Some of these warning signs include:

a). Cloud of Darkness: Somehow, you sense that something is wrong somewhere. You may not be able to lay hands on what exactly is wrong. But you can feel it. You can feel a cloud of darkness over the family.

Suddenly, children start having nightmares, crying in the night, or even getting sickly. Suddenly, finances become very hard for no reason at all. Suddenly, quarrels start happening between you and your spouse, and unnecessary strife and division begin to crop up in the home.

These are signs of a cloud of darkness. You need to embark on prayers to cleanse your home.

b). Loss of Zeal for the Things of God: The ultimate goal of every spiritual attack is to make people lose faith in God. If you find that the family's zeal for the Lord just started to derail, there may be an attack from the devil that has been unleashed on your home. Don't try to battle the situation with physical knowledge. Pray for your family and command the devil to vacate.

c). Cases of Nightmares: Suddenly, family members start reporting one nightmare after another. I don't mean unnecessary dreams born out of the busy-ness of the day. I mean that you can attest to some invasion that makes nearly everyone have nightmares almost every night. If this is happening, then your home is under attack. You need to pray a prayer of deliverance for your home.

d). Personal Discovery: If you discover after asking around that your home, office or property was a site for a major tragedy in the past, such as murder, accident, mass death, etc., or that it was a site for witchcraft meetings, occultic events, rituals, night club, satanic worship, etc., then you need to *'prayer-cleanse'* the home and environment as soon as possible.

e). Haunted: If you or anyone in the home is complaining of hearing unusual noises, discussions, movements, or strange things happening at night or odd hours of the day; maybe doors opening on their own, even when they were locked; or sounds of discussions going on, even when you can't see who is doing the meeting; don't play down on these things. Your home needs to be cleansed with prayers.

3. GENERATIONAL STRONGHOLDS

If you suspect that a situation happening in your home has some connection with your lineage, then a family deliverance or home cleansing prayer will do.

There are some families where the father has a problem with uncontrollable anger, his son seems to have been 'handed it', and the grandpa had the same problem? Or have you noticed that not only do you suffer from something such as persistent, irrational fears or depression, but your mother and her father also suffered from it as well?

Those are effects produced by inherited curses. They are beyond learned behaviors; they are bondages that must be consciously broken with prayer.

Another example of common symptoms of bloodline curses is family illnesses that seem to walk from one person down to the next, continual financial difficulties, mental problems, persistent, irrational fears and depression, etc. Family deliverance prayers is the way out when you are dealing with issues that have a generational connection.

OTHERS

Several other things may signal the need for deliverance prayers in the home. If you are reading this book, up to this point, the chances are that you are suspecting a need for deliverance in your home, or office, or environment. There's no harm in praying and commanding every form of evil influence to cease from your environment and asking the Lord, Jesus Christ, to rule and reign as King, forever and ever.

DON'T FORGET...

"Family deliverance prayers is the way out when you are dealing with issues that have a generational connection."

4

HOW TO INITIATE A HOME DELIVERANCE PRAYER

"Behold, I give unto you power to tread on serpents and scorpions, and over all the power of the enemy: and nothing shall by any means hurt you." - Luke 10:19

As someone who has witnessed Christ in the hinterlands of Africa, I can tell you that demonic possessions, oppressions and attacks are real. Unfortunately, Africa is not the only place where demons operate. They are everywhere. The Bible warns us to be alert because our enemy, the devil, is roaming about, everywhere, looking for whom to devour.

> ***"Lest Satan should get an advantage of us: for we are not ignorant of his devices."*** - 2 Cor. 2:11.

Demons are real. They can attack someone's home, business, marriage, children and ministry. Seek to understand how they work and stop them from your life and family; don't push the subject off as nonsense.

However, don't be afraid of demons. We have authority over the devil and all his powers. Once we discern a situation to be a demonic assault, we must exercise faith in dealing with them, not fear. Why? Because God already empowers us as Christians to bind and cast out demons, and the demons will obey. There is no special qualification required other than believing in Christ's love and victory over the devil.

You can stop the devil. Yes, you can. You can do it. Christ has already given you the power to do that. Rise and look at everything that is not right in your home and say, *"Okay, enough. I'm done accepting this situation. It's time to end it."*

What are the steps to carrying out a deliverance session in your home?

1. FORM A TEAM

If two of you shall agree on earth as touching anything that they shall ask, it shall be done for them of my Father which is in heaven. - Matt. 18:19

Two are better than one because they have a good return for their labor: If either of them falls down, one can help the other up. But pity anyone who falls and has no one to help them up.

Also, if two lies down together, they will keep warm. But how can one keep warm alone? Though one may be overpowered, two can defend themselves. A cord of three strands is not quickly broken. – Ecc. 4:9-12

There is power in a prayer of agreement. Family deliverance, home or property cleansing prayers are better done as a team of 2 persons or more. These other persons can be your spouse, children, brothers and sisters in Christ, and so on. What matters is that there is understanding and agreement.

2. FAST AND PRAY

Is not this the kind of fasting I have chosen: to loose the chains of injustice and untie the cords of the yoke, to set

the oppressed free and break every yoke? – Isaiah 58:6

You and your team should fast and pray before embarking on a home or property cleansing prayers, and while on the prayer sessions proper. You are embarking on a mission to dislodge the powers of darkness from your environment, so, a good spiritual preparation is necessary to keep your spirits alert.

Jesus said that there are stubborn demons that will try to resist our prayers, but with fasting, we can be adequately prepared to crush them. (Matthew 17:21).

Fasting increases the power of prayer several times over.

When you fast, ask the Holy Spirit to open your eyes to doorways that need to be removed. Humble yourself before God and receive direction to approach the prayer sessions.

There are different kinds of fasting. However, that is not the focus of this book. I usually encourage people to drink water when they are fasting. Whichever fasting you decide to do, whether it is 6-10 am, 6-12:00 noon, 6 pm-6 am, that's okay.

During this period, the chains of injustice against your life and family will be destroyed; the yoke on your life or any member of your family will be loosed; you and your family members will be set free from the oppression of the devil.

3. LOCATE DEMONIC DOORWAYS AND DEAL WITH THEM

Ask the Holy Spirit to show you the open doors that allowed evil spirits to come into your home, property and environment. He will show you things and areas that need to be addressed.

Some common examples of demonic doorways are porn, occult books, covenanted rings, objects used in witchcraft, willful disobedience to the Holy Spirit's leading, addictions, secret sins, satanic movies and even objects.

Some doorways may be sins, while others may be unknown objects somewhere in the house or property. As you pray and follow the leading of the Holy Spirit, He'll put it in your heart, areas that you may need to confess sins to the LORD or things to take away and destroy.

Be open to the Holy Spirit to show you what needs to be done, as this is crucial in the entire deliverance process. Look at this:

Many who had believed now came forward, confessing and disclosing their deeds. And a number of those who had practiced magic arts

brought their books and burned them in front of everyone.

When the value of the books was calculated, it came to fifty thousand drachmas.

So, the word of the Lord powerfully continued to spread and prevail - Acts 19:18-20

We cannot have deliverance if we harbor or keep the property of the devil with us.

4. PRAY IN THE NIGHT

The night hours are victory hours. What happens in the night times usually controls the fallouts of the day. That is why occult people mainly have their meetings in the night.

The Bible says: **"You will not fear the terror of night, nor the arrow that flies by day"**

(Psalm 91:5). That means that terrors are usually executed in the night times. You know why? Because *"Everyone who does evil hates the day and will not come into the light for fear that their deeds will be exposed* (John 3:30-Paraphrased).

Jesus said, *"But while men slept, his enemy came and sowed tares among the wheat, and went his way"* (Matthew 13:25).

Demonic forces exploit the night to sow tares in people's lives because they effortlessly get away without notice. But when we decide to watch and pray in the night, we can destroy whatever they have sown and release our blessings.

5. PRAY WITH THE WORD

This book will help you pray with the Word of God effectively. Your prayers will have more power when they are saturated with God's Word.

So, in praying the prayers in this book take time to read the scriptures that are recommended and personalize them. If you feel like praying some other way after reading a scripture before coming back to this outline, that's fine.

You may also need to pray outside the prayer points in this book. Yield to the Holy Spirit, gather prayer points and pray the Word until your deliverance is settled.

6. PRAY WITH AUTHORITY

Don't lay down half-asleep while praying. If possible, move around the property or environment you are claiming its deliverance. Move from room to room, corner to corner, pray and anoint everywhere as you do.

Do not just read out the prayers here only. The prayer points are guides. As you read out one, spend time praying it through with words the Holy Spirit puts in your mouth.

If you are baptized in the Holy Spirit, do not hesitate to pray in tongues whenever you are moved, even while you follow the prayer points and strategies in this book

7. PRAY WITH A NOTE

As you fast, pray and seek the Lord over your home, and demand deliverance, God will undoubtedly come through to you. He will speak to you and show you things you do not know. You will have revelations, dreams, trances, strong impressions or unusual insights while reading the Bible. These revelations will contain instructions you need to carry out, or areas you need to channel your prayers, or things you need to do. So be sure to be sensitive and write these revelations down, and quickly set about doing them.

While praying and demanding deliverance, you must recognize what God is saying and follow through. That's what gets prayers answered.

8. USE THE ANOINTING OIL

Get yourself a bottle of olive oil and ask someone with a higher spiritual authority to consecrate it for you. Then go into your prayers every night with it. At the end of each prayer session, anoint the said environment and declare it dedicated to the Lord. The oil is a symbol of the Holy Spirit used to invoke healing, protection, dedication, favor and divine enablement.

9. PRAY UNTIL IT IS SETTLED

Pray with this book until the situation is settled.

- Declare a seven-day fasting to wait on the Lord for deliverance from all attacks in your home and environment.

- Pray the prayers in the night, any time from midnight to 3:00 am.

- Write down every dream, idea, thought, or direction you receive during prayer and fasting and set out to do them.

- Do not stop praying until the mountains move. If after the first seven days, you don't feel relieved, continue praying. Declare another 3-day fasting and prayer. The battle against your life is serious. Don't go about it casually. Keep praying until there is a release in your spirit that the situation is under control. You will know this because your spirit will give you this assurance.

10. FOLLOW THESE PRAYER INSTRUCTIONS

- Spend a few minutes in praise and worship to the Lord before praying

- Confess any known sins

- Ask the Lord to bring to your memory the legal grounds or the doors that the forces of spiritual wickedness are using to gain entrance into your home, property and family.

- Where you have found the demonic doorways, remove them before praying.

- If you have any issue with anyone, forgive and ask God for grace to be free from anger and bitterness towards the people who have offended you.

- Believe in your prayers. Believe that your prayers will work.

DON'T FORGET...

"Don't be afraid of demons. We have authority over the devil and all his powers. Once we discern a situation to be a demonic assault, we must exercise faith in dealing with them, not fear."

DAY 1: PRAYERS FOR MERCY

CONFESSION

If my people, who are called by my name, will humble themselves and pray and seek my face and turn from their wicked ways, then I will hear from heaven, and I will forgive their sin and will heal their land

— 2 Chron. 7:14

....

=> Also read and declare Psalm 51

PRAYERS

Heavenly Father, I come to You on behalf of my family, home and this environment. I ask for forgiveness in any way we have sinned against You. Forgive us in Jesus name.

Today, O Lord, I confess the involvement of my family, parents, grandparents, and everyone who answered our surname and used this property. I confess their involvement in occult and witchcraft activities and plead for Your mercy.

May the Blood of Jesus Christ speak forgiveness and mercy in my family bloodline today and over this property and home, in Jesus name

---

Let the Blood of Jesus Christ flow into the roots of my family right now and cleanse us from all forms of unrighteousness.

Let the Blood of Jesus bring total separation from all forms of old and evil covenants.

And Let the Blood of Jesus Christ cancel and erase every satanic covenant speaking over this home and property, in the name of Jesus Christ.

O Lord, I pray, may every root of rebellion, witchcraft, and occultism, be uprooted from my family bloodline and this home and property, in Jesus name.

Today, I call forth the Blood of Jesus Christ that speaks better things than the blood of Abel.

Blood of Jesus Christ, speak forgiveness, healing, deliverance, and restoration over my family and home, in Jesus name.

Every evil voice speaking condemnation over my home, and over our property spiritually, hear the Word of God... **'There is therefore**

now no condemnation to those who are in Christ Jesus, who walk not after the flesh, but after the Spirit.' *(Rom. 8:1)*

I, therefore, command all voices speaking evil and condemnation against my home and belongings to cease right now, in Jesus name.

According to the Word of the Lord, I declare that there is therefore no more condemnation for my family.

The Blood of Jesus Christ speaks favor, love, salvation, freedom, and breakthrough, for this home and property, in Jesus name.

O Lord, baptize me and every member of this family with fresh fire from Heaven. Let Your Spirit empower us from today onwards to live and serve You, in truth and Spirit, in Jesus Name.

From now onwards, I pray, Lord, cause us to rely on the strength and energy that You provide alone. I pray that everything we do within this family unit, property, and environment will bring You glory through the One who lives in us – Your Son, Jesus Christ, in Jesus name.

DAY 2: ERECT A NEW ALTAR

CONFESSION

Love the Lord your God with all your heart and with all your soul and with all your strength.

These commandments that I give you today are to be on your hearts. Impress them on your children. Talk about them when you sit at home and when you walk along the road, when you lie down and when you get up.

Tie them as symbols on your hands and bind them on your foreheads. Write them on the doorframes of your houses and on your gates - Deut. 6:5-9 (NIV)

PRAYERS

Heavenly Father, I stand before You this day and claim this home, property and environment for You.

I claim every member of this home for You, Lord.

I decree and declare that we belong to You and to You alone, in Jesus name.

From this day, Lord, we enter a covenant to seek You in this house, property and environment. Help and guide us in our desire to be Your ambassadors in this place.

I ask that Your Spirit will take charge of the lives of everyone connected to this household from this day onwards, in Jesus name.

Lord Jesus Christ, no one can come to You except the Father draws him. (John 6:44).

Therefore, through the Holy Spirit, Jesus, draw every member of this household to Yourself.

It is written in Proverbs 21:1 that the heart of man is in the hand of God.

Even so, Lord, the hearts of every member of this household is in Your hand. The hearts of everyone living in this place and those who will live in this place later is in Your hands.

Lord, I ask that You empower us all, today, tomorrow and forever, to seek after You and You alone, in this family, property and environment, through the Holy Spirit, in Jesus name.

Father Lord, I ask You to help each member of our family (name them) to be completely humble and gentle in our interactions with each other; and to be patient, bearing with one another's faults in love – even when we're tired, frustrated, angry, or hurt. Please help us, Father, to make every effort to remain united in the Spirit in this home. Bind us together in peace, in Jesus name.

Gracious Father in Heaven, help us (name your family members) to love each other fervently. Grow our love so deep that it is able and willing to overcome and forgive a multitude of sins, in Jesus Name.

King of kings and Lord of lords, Jesus Christ, I dedicate this home to You from today. Rule and rein from now till eternity. Be the Lord and Savior of this home and property henceforth, in Jesus name.

I speak to every evil altar in and around this environment to be destroyed by fire from above right now, in Jesus name.

Every messenger of the devil stationed in and around this home and property, I place an arrest order against you all right now. I command you all to be bundled into the abyss henceforth, and never return, in Jesus name.

I decree and declare that this home and property is the Lord's. Every member of this home and everyone who will ever visit this property belongs to God, in Jesus name.

I declare this property sanctified by the Blood of Jesus Christ.

As I invoke the Blood of Jesus Christ this moment, I declare that the spiritual and physical foundation of this property and home is sanctified and delivered from all evil attachments, defilements, and covenants, in Jesus name

---

Blood of Jesus Christ

Blood of Jesus Christ

Blood of Jesus Christ

Blood of Jesus Christ

Blood of Jesus Christ

Blood of Jesus Christ

Blood of Jesus Christ

Cleanse this home and property from all forms of evil and speak for this home and property, in Jesus name.

As Jacob built an altar at Bethel to serve as a memorial for God revealing Himself to him, (Gen.35:6-7) ...

Today, I spiritually erect an altar in this home and property henceforth.

From now onwards, Lord, reveal Yourself to every member of this home and property.

May Your Angels station in the four corners of this home and property with swords of fire and keep off evil forever and ever. May they minister to us and help us stay safe, and sound, all the days of our lives, in Jesus name.

Henceforth, I decree that this home and property shall be a source of light and salvation to all nations, in Jesus name.

DAY 3: ADDRESS THE POWERS

CONFESSION

No weapon that is formed against thee shall prosper, and every tongue that shall rise against thee in judgment thou shalt condemn. This is the heritage of the servants of the LORD, and their righteousness is of me, saith the LORD. – Isaiah 54:17.

PRAYERS

O LORD my Father, today, I dethrone every evil throne that has been raised against this home and property. Every force of wickedness working against any member of this family, be destroyed in Jesus name.

Every power assigned to cause rebellion and destruction in this home, perish by fire right now, in Jesus name.

I set free any member of this family under the bondage of the devil; I command them to regain their freedom in all aspects of their lives, in Jesus name.

Every negative statement and curse against this household and property, be erased by fire, from today onwards, in Jesus name.

I replace any curse working against us before now with the blessings of God. Where the enemy decreed death, I decree life. Where they decreed sickness, I decree healing and divine health. Where they decreed failure and stagnation, I decree prosperity and divine favor, in Jesus name.

I condemn every tongue speaking evil against my life, my household and our property today. I bring them to judgment, and I command them to tear apart, in Jesus name.

Every strange voice speaking against this family and property, spiritually, physically, and otherwise, I command you to cease today, and be destroyed, in Jesus name

---

Every monitoring demon assigned from the pit of hell to harass this household and property, I bind you all right now and command you all to get back into the abyss and never return, in Jesus name.

This home belongs to the LORD Jesus. This property belongs to the LORD Jesus.

Therefore, any evil spirit claiming ownership and residence in this place, pack your loads and leave right now, and go back to the abyss where you belong, in Jesus name.

Any man or woman sitting down to hold a meeting against me and my family, wherever they are, O Lord, I command fire from heaven to scatter them, in Jesus name.

I detach myself and all the members of my family from every negative attachment that is not bringing glory to God.

By the Blood of Jesus Christ, I decree that we have victory; we have been delivered to walk in righteousness, in Jesus name.

Every evil seed planted in this family (name it), I command you to die by fire.

Whatever has been programmed to cause discord and confusion in this family and property, I command them to be destroyed henceforth, in Jesus name.

O Lord, I pray that the Blood of Jesus will be upon this whole house and surroundings and wash away all evildoers and evil influences causing distress, pain and suffering to this house, in Jesus name.

From today, Lord, may our financial needs be met according to the blessings of God through Jesus Christ, our Lord and Savior, in Jesus name

---

I raise a banner of victory over this place. I decree that this place is sanctified and dedicated to the Lord, in Jesus name.

(Move around and anoint the property and house)

As I anoint this house, I decree a total cleansing from evil.

Every yoke of the devil causing oppression, heaviness, lack, strife, nightmares, fear, poverty, rebellion, sickness and death, I command them to be broken right now, in Jesus name.

I command total healing and restoration over this house and its dwellers from today.

I dedicate this property, this house, this building, this environment, every part of this place to the Lord.

Henceforth, I decree that the light of God will continue to shine in this place, forever and ever, in Jesus name.

I decree that we shall never labor in vain. The works of our hands shall be fruitful from this day forward, in Jesus name.

May those who have planned evil for this property, house and family, be disgraced

May the evil they have planned against us be upon them, for it is written in Psalm 94: 3 that, 'He has brought back their wickedness upon them And will destroy them in their evil; the Lord our God will destroy them, in Jesus name.

The peace and prosperity of the Lord is upon this place henceforth. Out of this place shall proceed forth greatness and testimony, victory and joy, forever and ever, in Jesus name.

DAY 4: SALVATION PRAYERS

CONFESSION

2 Peter 3:9 - *The Lord is not slack concerning His promise, as some count slackness, but is longsuffering toward us, not willing that any should perish but that all should come to repentance.*

1 Timothy 2:3-4 - *This is good, and pleases God our Savior, who wants all people to be saved and to come to a knowledge of the truth.*

Acts 16:31 – *I believe in the Lord Jesus; I will be saved, along with everyone in my household."*

PRAYERS

O Lord my Father, I present my family before you today. It is not Your will that anyone should perish.

Therefore, Lord, I ask that You visit all my family members this day with Your saving power, in Jesus name.

Father, I pray, let (mention names) be convicted of Your Love and be drawn to You, in Jesus name.

Every spirit of rebellion and disobedience in the life of............. I bind and cast them out, and send them to the abyss, in Jesus name.

I command all my family members (mention names) .... be set free from the power of sin right now, in Jesus name.

Wherever you are...................I command you to receive Jesus as your Lord and personal Savior. Receive a meek and humble spirit right now, in Jesus name.

Dear Holy Spirit, take over my family from today. Take over the life of (mention names) and establish them in the knowledge of Christ, in Jesus name.

O Lord, my Father, give .... the power and wisdom to resist sin and temptations henceforth, in Jesus name.

O Lord, baptize (mention names) with the Holy Spirit. Let Your power from above descend on them wherever they are right now, in Jesus name.

Every spirit of resistance, I cast you out of (mention names), in Jesus name.

Thank You, Lord, for visiting (mention names) with Your saving power, in Jesus name.

DAY 5: GUIDANCE AND FAVOR

CONFESSION

Psalms 32:8 – God will instruct me and teach me in the way which I shall go; He will guide me with His eyes.

Proverbs 3:5-6 - I trust in the Lord with all my heart; I do not lean unto my own understanding. In all my ways, I will acknowledge Him, and he shall direct my paths.

John 16:13 – The Holy Spirit is the Spirit of truth. He is come to guide me into all truth. He does not speak of himself; whatsoever He says to me is what heaven has decided for me. And He will show you things to come.

Isaiah 30:21 – *My ears shall hear a word behind me, saying, this is the way, walk ye in it, when I turn to the right hand, and when I turn to the left.*

James 1:5-6 – *As I ask and seek God for wisdom, God, who gives to all men liberally, and upbraids not, shall give me wisdom and I shall know what to do going forward.*

PRAYERS

O Lord, I thank You because it is Your desire to guide us. Thank You because You have given us the Holy Spirit to guide and lead us into all truth. May you be praised forever and ever in Jesus name.

Father, there are many desires and plans in our hearts. But only Your counsel shall stand. I, therefore, surrender all our plans before You this day and ask that the Holy Spirit will guide us in Jesus name.

Cause us, Lord, to lose interest in any project and plan that is a spiritual trap, that is not part of Your plans for our lives, in Jesus name.

Today, Lord, I ask for wisdom for my life and family. Teach me to walk in the path ordained for me, in Jesus name.

Whatever is blocking my spiritual ears from hearing from You, Lord, let it be destroyed in Jesus name.

Holy Spirit, I invite You into my life and family. Come and be our Guide. Come and be our teacher. Come and be our instructor, in Jesus name.

O Lord, today, I speak favor into my life and family.

According to Your Word in **Psalms 5:12,** *Lord, You will bless us and surround us with favor as with a shield.*

You do not withhold good things from Your children according to Psalm 84:11.

Thank You because your Word is yea and amen.

Therefore, I declare that everything that makes life great is our portion.

From now onwards, men and women are working for our good.

My Family is experiencing favor all around, in Jesus name.

For thou, Lord, wilt bless the righteous; with favor wilt thou compass him as with a shield (Psalm 5:12)

.....

O Lord, encompass me with Your favor like a shield.

Cause me to be at the right place and at the right time, in Jesus name

---

Every attack of men and women, humans or spirits, against my life, against my marriage, and against my finances, be canceled today, in the name of Jesus Christ.

Today, I decree and declare that…

I have favor with God.

I will find favor with men and women.

I will find favor with kings and princes

I will find favor with my spouse

I will find favor with everyone I meet henceforth, in the name of Jesus.

I declare that God will arise and have mercy on us, for the time to favor us has come; yeah, this is my time of favor (Psalm 102:13).

I declare that by God's favor...

I receive answers to every prayer I have made in the past.

And I receive a supernatural harvest for every seed I have sown in the past, in the name of Jesus.

The Bible says that *Joseph found favor in Potiphar's eyes and became his attendant. Potiphar put him in charge of his household, and he entrusted him to his care, everything he owned.*

I declare today, Lord,

Wherever I work and do business, I have favor with people.

I find favor in my place of work.

I am celebrated in my ministry and place of divine assignment, in Jesus name.

In the name of Jesus Christ, I decree that I find favor with anyone connected to my financial breakthrough.

When God wants to help a man, He sends a man.

Sometimes, our helpers are around, but because our eyes are blinded, we are not seeing them.

Father, Lord, open my eyes to recognize and be connected to anyone You have sent to be a blessing to my life and destiny.

And may the eyes of anyone supernaturally designed to be a helper to my destiny and life be opened to recognize their assignment in my life, in Jesus name.

As God was with Joseph, He is with me. He has not changed. He is the same yesterday, today and forever.

I, therefore, declare that I am finding favor with my bosses, supervisors, colleagues, and clients, in the name of Jesus Christ.

Today, I banish the spirit of hatred, curses, and offensive jealousy and envy against me, in the mighty name of Jesus Christ.

From today,

I decree that God is fighting my battles.

I am a victor and not a victim.

I am going forward, from glory to glory.

Whatever I lay my hands upon and whatever I touch will prosper, for God says that I am like a tree planted by the sides of the river, in Jesus name.

I decree that...

I have favor with kings in high places.

I have favor with everyone I work and do business with.

I have favor with the government, in the name of Jesus.

God's favor is at work in my life, henceforth.

I, therefore, command that every contract I have applied for, every tender I have made, wherever my CV is, in the name of Jesus Christ, may they receive special attention and be approved, in Jesus name.

I decree that I am not lazy.

I am not idle and will never be idle

I am a person of value.

I have exceptional skills and the tongue of the learned.

I make things happen

Therefore, I will stand before kings and princes;

I will offer my services before great people, and not before mean and ordinary people, in Jesus name.

God is blessing me with favor and honor. No good thing will He withhold from me. With Him, I am a majority.

I receive grace to carry out every business idea God is giving me and to execute my job with the excellency of wisdom from above, in Jesus name.

From this day forward...

Favor will speak for me in the morning, in the afternoon, in the evening, and all the days of my life, in the name of Jesus Christ.

I decree that I will no longer remain at one spot; I will no longer stay stagnant.

I curse the spirit of delay and stagnation, and I cast them into the abyss.

I receive divine touch that accelerates my efforts and commands speedy results in the works of my hands, in the name of Jesus Christ.

Every wrong person stationed in my life, preventing the right persons from showing up, I chase them away in the name of Jesus Christ.

From today, I begin to attract the right people into my life and destiny.

I begin to attract the right connections, and breakthroughs, in Jesus name.

In the name of Jesus Christ, I declare that...

I have the spirit of creativity.

I create and invent things.

I provide smart solutions to problems.

I find ways where others are stuck.

Light is continually shining in my ways, and people are learning how to do things from me.

Thank You, Jesus, for answered prayers.

Thank You for causing everyone and everything to work for my good and the good of my finances.

Thank You for causing people to want to help and support me in the works of my hand.

Thank you for blessing me with the spirit of creativity.

Thank You for causing me to make the right decisions at all times, in Jesus name, I pray.

Amen.

DAY 6: PROTECTION

CONFESSION

2 Thessalonians 3:3 - *The Lord is faithful, who shall establish us, and keep us from evil.*

2 Timothy 4:18 - *The Lord shall deliver us from every evil work and will preserve us unto his heavenly kingdom: to Him be glory forever and ever.*

PRAYERS

Because we dwell in the secret place of the most High, we shall abide under the shadow of the Almighty.

We will say of the Lord, He is our refuge and my fortress: our God; in him will we trust. Surely, he shall deliver us from the snare of the fowler, and from the noisome pestilence.

God will cover us with his feathers, and under his wings shall we find refuge. God's truth shall be our shield and buckler.

We shall not be afraid for the terror by night; nor for the arrow that flies by day; Nor for the pestilence that walks in darkness; nor for the destruction that happens in the afternoon.

Even if a thousand falls at our side, and ten thousand at our right hand, it shall not come near us, in Jesus name.

God is our refuge and fortress. He will keep us safe at all times; only with our eyes shall we behold and see the reward of the wicked and the events in the world.

There shall no evil befall us; neither shall any disease come near our house.

God has given His angels charge over us to keep us in all our ways. They are bearing us up in their hands; we will not dash our foot against a stone.

We shall tread upon the lions and the serpents: We will trample the dragons under our feet.

God will deliver us and set us on high and satisfy us with long life, in Jesus name.

DAY 7: DIVINE PROVISION

CONFESSION

Matthew 6:26 - *Behold the fowls of the air: they sow not, neither do they reap, nor gather into barns, yet my heavenly Father feeds them. And I am much better than them. If God provides for them, He provides much more for us.*

2 Peter 1:3 – *Through His promises, God has given us all things pertaining to life and godliness. Through the knowledge of His promises, we are called unto glory and virtue.*

Philippians 4:19 - *God shall supply all our need according to his riches in glory by Christ Jesus.*

PRAYERS

O Lord, my God, because You are our shepherd, we shall not be in want. You will lead us in green pastures,

My Family and I shall always have all-sufficiency. We shall share with many and not borrow.

Every spirit of worry and anxiety, I bind and cast you into the abyss.

I declare that we are not anxious for anything, because God is our support. Henceforth, our needs are met supernaturally every day, in Jesus name.

If God takes care of the birds of the air, how much more me and my family.

God is taking care of us. We have all that we need at all times. Doors and supplies are open before us. We have abundance in Christ Jesus, in Jesus name.

Today, I declare that I am confident that God, who started a good work in us, will bring it unto perfection (**Philippians 1:6**)*.*

We shall never be stranded in this family again. We are moving forward and glorifying God, in Jesus name.

Father, Lord, baptize us with the spirit of contentment. Let the power of greed be destroyed in our lives and family, in Jesus name.

God's thoughts and plans for me and my family is to have great peace and a great future.

I, therefore, decree that our tomorrow is secured. We have peace on all sides, in Jesus name.

When others are complaining about being cast down, we shall be saying there is a lifting up. This is the Word of God (Job 22:29). And it is the heritage of this family.

Almighty Father, thank you. You are forever exalted in my life and family, in Jesus name.

GOD

BLESS

YOU

CONTACT US

Thank you for reading this book. I believe you have been blessed. Please consider giving this book a review on Amazon.

I also invite you to check out our website at www.BetterLifeWorld.org and consider joining our newsletter, which we send out once in a while with great tips, testimonies and revelations from God's Word for a victorious living.

Feel free to drop us your prayer request. We will join faith with you, and God's power will be released in your life and the issue in question.

OTHER BOOKS BY THE SAME AUTHOR

Latest Books

31 Days in the School of Faith

31 Days With the Heroes of Faith

31 Days With the Holy Spirit

31 Days With Jesus

31 Days in the Parables

None of These Diseases

I Will Arise and Shine

Psalm 91: His Secret Place, His Shadow, and His Protection

All Books

Prayer Retreat: 21 Days Devotional With Over 500 Prayers & Declarations to Destroy Stubborn Demonic Problems.

HEALING PRAYERS & CONFESSIONS

200 Violent Prayers for Deliverance, Healing, and Financial Breakthrough.

Hearing God's Voice in Painful Moments

Healing Prayers: Prophetic Prayers that Brings Healing

Healing WORDS: Daily Confessions & Declarations to Activate Your Healing.

Prayers That Break Curses and Spells and Release Favors and Breakthroughs.

120 Powerful Night Prayers That Will Change Your Life Forever.

How to Pray for Your Children Everyday

How to Pray for Your Family

Daily Prayer Guide

Make Him Respect You: 31 Very Important Relationship Intelligence for Women to Make their Men Respect them.

How to Cast Out Demons from Your Home, Office & Property

Praying Through the Book of Psalms

The Students' Prayer Book

How to Pray and Receive Financial Miracle

Powerful Prayers to Destroy Witchcraft Attacks.

Deliverance from Marine Spirits

Deliverance From Python Spirit

Anger Management God's Way

How God Speaks to You

Deliverance of the Mind

20 Commonly Asked Questions About Demons

Praying the Promises of God

When God Is Silent! What to Do When Prayer Seems Unanswered or Delayed

I SHALL NOT DIE: Prayers to Overcome the Spirit and Fear of Death.

Praise Warfare

Prayers to Find a Godly Spouse

How to Exercise Authority Over Sickness

Under His Shadow: Praying the Promises of God for Protection (Book 2).

Audio Books

120 Powerful Night Prayers that Will Change Your Life

28 Days of Praise Challenge: Dealing With Your Fears and Battles Through Intentional Praise

Anger Management God's Way: Bible Ways to Control Your Emotions, Get Healed of Hurts & Respond to Offenses ...Plus Powerful Daily Prayers to Overcome Bad Anger Permanently

By His Stripes: God's Promises & Prayers for Healing

Deliverance of the mind: Powerful Prayers to Deal With Mind Control, Fear, Anxiety, Depression, Anger and Other Negative Emotions.

Healing Words: Daily Confessions & Declarations to Activate Your Healing

How God Speaks to You: An ABC Guide to Hearing the Voice of God & Following His Direction for Your Life

How to Exercise Authority Over Sickness: Authoritative Prayers and Declarations for Personal Healing, and Healing of Your Loved Ones

How to Meditate on God's Word: Fast and Easy Ways to Practice Intentional Bible Meditation and Grow in Faith, Worship, and Prayer

Prayers to Find a Godly Spouse: Meditations, Prophetic Declarations and Biblical Foundation for Finding a Life Partner

Praying the Promises of God for Daily Blessings and Breakthrough

Take it By Force: 200 Violent Prayers for Deliverance, Healing and Financial Breakthrough

Under His Shadow: God's Promises and Prayers for Protection

When God Is Silent: What to Do When Prayers Seems Unanswered or Delayed

Beside the Still Waters: God's Promises and Prayers for Guidance and Direction | Learn to Know the Will of God & Make Right Decisions

Less Panic More Hope: God's Promises and Prayers to Overcome Fear, Anxiety, and Depression – Scriptures and Prayers for Mental Health

How to Pray for Your Family: Plus Over 70 Prayers for Your Family's Salvation, Healing, Restoration, and Breakthrough

Prayers that Break Curses: Everything You Need to Know About Curses, and Powerful Prayers to Stop All Kinds of Curses

20 Commonly Asked Questions About Demons: Answers You Need to Bind and Cast Out Demons, Heal the Sick, and Experience Breakthrough

Deliverance by Fire: 21 Days of Intensive Word Immersion, and Fire Prayers for Total Healing, Deliverance, Breakthrough, and Divine Intervention.

Command Your Money: Powerful Keys to Provoke Financial Breakthrough | 10 Simple Actions of Faith That Will Provoke Financial Breakthrough for Anyone in 30 Days or Less

NOTES

Made in the USA
Monee, IL
26 December 2021